# FAMILY MEALS

CHANCELLOR
PRESS

# CONTENTS

First published in Great Britain in 1980

This edition published in 1994 by Chancellor Press
an imprint of Reed Consumer Books Limited
Michelin House, 81 Fulham Road, London SW3 6RB
and Auckland, Melbourne, Singapore and Toronto

Reprinted 1994

Copyright © 1980 Reed International Books Limited

ISBN 1 85152 512 2

A CIP catalogue record for this book is available from the British Library

Produced by Mandarin Offset
Printed and bound in Hong Kong

# INTRODUCTION

The term 'family meals' is all too frequently associated with plain, unexciting meals. Although busy mothers only have limited time to spend in the kitchen, there are plenty of quick-to-prepare, inexpensive dishes which are just that little bit different and suitable for all the family.

Here you will find a tempting selection of recipes, ranging from tasty versions of well-known favourites, such as hamburgers and savoury cauliflower cheese, to more adventurous recipes for chilled soups, pâtés and mouth-watering desserts.

NOTES

Standard spoon measurements are used in all recipes
1 tablespoon = one 15 ml spoon
1 teaspoon = one 5 ml spoon
All spoon measures are level.

Fresh herbs are used unless otherwise stated. If unobtainable substitute a bouquet garni of the equivalent dried herbs, or use dried herbs instead but halve the quantities stated.

Use freshly ground black pepper where pepper is specified.

If fresh yeast is unobtainable, substitute dried yeast but use only half the recommended quantity and follow the manufacturer's instructions for reconstituting.

Ovens should be preheated to the specified temperature.

For all recipes, quantities are given in both metric and imperial measures. Follow either set but not a mixture of both, because they are not interchangeable.

# Carrot and Orange Soup

25 g (1 oz) butter
1 tablespoon oil
500 g (1 lb) carrots,
   sliced
2 medium onions,
   chopped
20 g (¾ oz) plain
   flour
900 ml (1½ pints)
   chicken stock
grated rind and juice
   of ½ orange
juice of ½ lemon
salt and pepper
croûtons to garnish
   (optional)

Heat the butter and oil in a saucepan, add the carrot and onion and fry until softened. Sprinkle in the flour and cook, stirring, for 1 minute. Remove from the heat and gradually stir in the stock. Return to the heat and bring to the boil, stirring.

Add the orange rind and juice, the lemon juice, salt and pepper to taste. Cover and simmer for 30 minutes.

Cool slightly, then work in an electric blender until smooth or rub through a sieve. Heat through before serving, with croûtons if liked.

**Serves 4 to 6**

NOTE: To make croûtons, fry small bread cubes in butter until crisp.

# Cold Cucumber Soup

1 large cucumber
3 x 150 g (5 oz)
  cartons natural
  low-fat yogurt
142 ml (5 fl oz)
  fresh sour cream
salt and pepper
1-2 tablespoons finely
  chopped mint
mint sprigs to garnish

Peel the cucumber and grate coarsely. Mix with the yogurt, sour cream, and salt and pepper to taste. Chill for about 2 hours.

Stir in chopped mint to taste. Pour into chilled soup bowls and top with mint sprigs to garnish.
**Serves 6**

# Quick Mushroom Soup

50 g (2 oz) butter
40 g (1½ oz) flour
600 ml (1 pint)
  chicken stock
300 ml (½ pint)
  milk
250 g (8 oz)
  mushrooms, finely
  chopped
1 clove garlic,
  crushed (optional)
salt and pepper
1 tablespoon lemon
  juice
1 tablespoon chopped
  parsley
114 ml (4 fl oz)
  single cream
paprika to garnish

Melt the butter in a saucepan, then stir in the flour. Cook, stirring, for 1 minute, then gradually stir in the stock and milk. Bring to the boil, stirring constantly.

Add the mushrooms, garlic, if using, salt and pepper to taste, and lemon juice. Simmer for 5 minutes, then stir in the parsley and cream. Reheat gently; do not allow to boil. Pour into individual soup bowls and sprinkle with paprika.

**Serves 6**

# Pea and Ham Soup

125 g (4 oz) dried
   green peas, soaked
   overnight
1 small knuckle of
   bacon, soaked
   overnight
1.5 litres (2½ pints)
   water
50 g (2 oz) butter
1 onion, chopped
2 potatoes, sliced
2 celery sticks, sliced
salt and pepper

Drain the peas and bacon knuckle,
then place in a large saucepan with
the fresh water and bring to the boil.
Cover and simmer for 2 hours.

Melt the butter in a frying pan,
add the onion, potato and celery and
fry gently until softened.

Remove the bacon knuckle from
the pan, cool slightly, then remove
the meat from the bone, discarding
the fat. Dice the meat and set aside.

Add the fried vegetables to the
peas, cover and simmer until all the
vegetables are tender. Cool slightly,
then work in an electric blender until
smooth or rub through a sieve.
Return to the pan, add the reserved
bacon and salt and pepper to taste
and heat through before serving.
**Serves 6 to 8**

# Vegetable Soup

50-125 g (2-4 oz)
  butter
2 rashers streaky
  bacon, derinded
  and chopped
2 onions, chopped
2 large leeks,
  chopped
1 parsnip, chopped
2 carrots, chopped
1 potato, chopped
900 ml (1½ pints)
  beef stock
1 x 227 g (8 oz) can
  tomatoes
2 bay leaves
¼ teaspoon dried
  thyme
1 tablespoon chopped
  parsley
salt and pepper

Melt 50 g (2 oz) of the butter in a
large saucepan, add the bacon and fry
gently. Add the vegetables and cook
until they are softened, adding more
butter if necessary.

Pour in the stock and add the
tomatoes with their juice, herbs and
salt and pepper to taste. Bring to the
boil, cover and simmer for 30 to 45
minutes, or until the vegetables are
cooked.

Allow the soup to cool a little,
then remove the bay leaves. Work in
an electric blender until smooth or
rub through a sieve. Return to the
pan to heat through before serving.
**Serves 4 to 6**

10

# Leek and Potato Soup

50 g (2 oz) butter
1 tablespoon oil
6 leeks, sliced
4 medium potatoes,
    sliced
1.2 litres (2 pints)
    chicken stock
salt and pepper
pinch of grated
    nutmeg
170 ml (6 fl oz)
    single cream
chopped chives to
    garnish (optional)

Heat the butter and oil in a saucepan, add the leeks and fry for about 10 minutes or until softened. Add the potatoes, stock, salt and pepper to taste, and nutmeg. Cover and simmer for about 30 minutes or until the vegetables are tender. Cool slightly, then work in an electric blender until smooth or rub through a sieve.

If the soup is to be served hot, return to the saucepan, add the cream and heat through; do not allow to boil. Adjust the seasoning if necessary.

If serving cold, stir in the cream and chill. Check the seasoning and garnish with chopped chives, if liked.
**Serves 6**

# French Onion Soup

50 g (2 oz) butter
4 large onions, sliced
1½ tablespoons flour
900 ml (1½ pints)
   beef stock
salt and pepper
TO GARNISH:
4-6 slices French
   bread
50 g (2 oz) Cheddar
   cheese, grated

Melt the butter in a saucepan, add the onions and fry until softened and just beginning to colour. Sprinkle in the flour and cook, stirring, until beginning to brown. Remove from the heat and gradually add the stock. Return to the heat and bring to the boil, stirring. Add salt and pepper to taste and simmer for 30 minutes.

Pour into individual ovenproof bowls and float a slice of French bread in each. Top with cheese and place under a preheated grill until golden and bubbling.

**Serves 4 to 6**

# Lettuce Soup

50 g (2 oz) butter
250 g (8 oz) lettuce
   leaves, shredded
1 medium onion,
   finely chopped
600 ml (1 pint)
   chicken stock
salt and pepper
1 teaspoon sugar
croûtons to garnish
   (see page 6)
BÉCHAMEL SAUCE:
300 ml (½ pint)
   milk
1 onion
4 cloves
4 peppercorns
pinch of grated
   nutmeg
25 g (1 oz) butter
25 g (1 oz) flour

Melt the butter in a saucepan, add the lettuce and onion and cook gently for 10 minutes, stirring occasionally. Add the stock, salt and pepper to taste and sugar. Simmer, covered, for 30 minutes.

Meanwhile, make the sauce. Pour the milk into a saucepan, add the onion stuck with the cloves, the peppercorns and nutmeg. Bring to the boil slowly, then turn off the heat, cover the pan and leave to stand for 15 minutes. Strain.

Melt the butter in a small pan and stir in the flour. Cook, stirring, for 1 minute then remove from the heat and allow to cool. Gradually add the hot milk, then return to the heat and bring to the boil, stirring constantly.

Add the sauce to the lettuce, mixing well, and simmer for 10 minutes. Cool slightly, then work in an electric blender until smooth or rub through a sieve.

Return to the pan and heat through or, if serving cold, chill. Check the seasoning and garnish with croûtons.

**Serves 4 to 6**

# Chilled Spanish Tomato Soup

500 g (1 lb)
  tomatoes, skinned
  and chopped
1 medium onion,
  chopped
1 small green pepper,
  cored, seeded and
  chopped
1 clove garlic, crushed
1 tablespoon wine
  vinegar
2 tablespoons olive
  oil
2 tablespoons lemon
  juice
1 slice white bread,
  crusts removed
300 ml (½ pint)
  chicken stock
salt and pepper
TO GARNISH:
diced cucumber
croûtons (see page 6)

Place all the ingredients in an electric blender and blend for a few seconds until smooth. Turn into a bowl, cover and chill thoroughly.

Serve the diced cucumber and croûtons as a garnish, in separate dishes.

**Serves 4**

# Corn-on-the-cob

4 fresh corn cobs
1 tablespoon sugar
TO SERVE:
salt and pepper
125 g (4 oz) butter

Strip the husks off the corn and remove all the silky threads. Place in a large shallow saucepan containing just enough boiling water to cover them. Add the sugar. (Do not add salt during cooking as this tends to toughen corn.) Return to the boil and boil for 5 to 6 minutes until tender. Drain thoroughly.

Place the cobs on individual serving dishes and insert special cob holders, small skewers or strong toothpicks at either end of each one for holding. Serve immediately with plenty of salt, pepper and butter.
**Serves 4**

# Melon and Grapefruit Starter

1 honeydew melon
500 g (1 lb) tomatoes
½ cucumber
½ x 539 g (19 oz)
   can grapefruit
   segments, drained
1 tablespoon snipped
   chives to garnish
DRESSING:
3 tablespoons lemon
   juice
6 tablespoons
   vegetable oil
salt and pepper

Quarter the melon, remove the seeds and skin, and cut the flesh into cubes. Skin and quarter the tomatoes; cut the quarters in half if they are large. Peel the cucumber and cut into cubes.

Mix together the melon, tomatoes, cucumber and grapefruit in a serving dish.

Shake the dressing ingredients together in a screw-top jar and pour over the salad. Sprinkle with chives and chill for 1 hour.
**Serves 8**

# Greek Cod's Roe Pâté

50 g (2 oz) fresh
   white breadcrumbs
250 g (8 oz) smoked
   cod's roe, skinned
1½ tablespoons
   lemon juice
1 clove garlic, crushed
150 ml (¼ pint)
   olive oil
½ teaspoon tomato
   purée
pepper

Soak the breadcrumbs in water to cover for 10 minutes. Place in a sieve and press with the back of a spoon to remove any excess water.

Place all the ingredients, with pepper to taste, in an electric blender and work until smooth. Spoon into a serving dish.

Serve with toast or pitta bread.
**Serves 4**

# Chicken Liver Pâté

125 g (4 oz) butter
250 g (8 oz) chicken
   livers, trimmed
1 small onion, finely
   chopped
1 clove garlic,
   crushed
1 tablespoon brandy
   or dry sherry
salt and pepper
grated nutmeg
1 bay leaf

Melt half the butter in a frying pan. Add the livers, onion and garlic, cover and cook gently for 5 minutes. Remove from the heat, cool slightly, then add the brandy or sherry, with salt, pepper and nutmeg to taste. Work in an electric blender until smooth.

Spoon into a small serving dish and place the bay leaf on top. Melt the remaining butter and pour over the pâté. Chill until firm. Serve with toast.
**Serves 4**

# FISH

## Mackerel in Horseradish Sauce

4 medium mackerel
2 teaspoons cornflour
3 tablespoons
    creamed
    horseradish
2 tablespoons lemon
    juice
4 tablespoons white
    wine
salt and pepper
cucumber slices to
    garnish (optional)

Cut the heads off the fish, then gut them and remove the backbones. Place the fish, skin side down, in a greased casserole.

Blend the cornflour into the horseradish, then gradually add the lemon juice and wine. Season with salt and pepper to taste and pour over the fish. Cover and cook in a preheated moderate oven, 160°C (325°F), Gas Mark 3, for 30 minutes, until tender.

Garnish with cucumber slices, if liked, before serving.

**Serves 4**

# Cheesy Cod

4 cod steaks
75 g (3 oz) Cheddar
  cheese, grated
1 teaspoon
  Worcestershire
  sauce
1 tablespoon milk
salt and pepper
parsley sprigs to
  garnish

Place the cod steaks on a greased grill pan and grill on one side for 4 to 5 minutes. Mix the remaining ingredients together, with salt and pepper to taste.

Turn the fish over and spread the uncooked side with the cheese mixture. Reduce the heat slightly and grill for about 5 minutes or until the fish is cooked and the topping golden and bubbling. Garnish with parsley.

**Serves 4**

# Fish Pie

500 g (1 lb) cod or
 haddock fillets
salt and pepper
1 tablespoon oil
50 g (2 oz) butter
1 large onion,
 chopped
1 x 397 g (14 oz)
 can tomatoes
1 clove garlic,
 crushed (optional)
125 g (4 oz)
 mushrooms, sliced
½ teaspoon dried
 thyme
1 teaspoon sugar
500 g (1 lb)
 potatoes, boiled
2 tablespoons milk
2 tablespoons grated
 Cheddar cheese

Place the fish in a saucepan with
enough cold water to cover. Season
to taste with salt and pepper. Bring
to simmering point and simmer for
10 minutes.

Meanwhile, heat the oil and half
the butter in a frying pan, add the
onion and fry gently for 5 minutes or
until softened. Stir in the tomatoes
with their juice, garlic, if using,
mushrooms and thyme and cook for
5 minutes. Add the sugar and salt
and pepper to taste.

Drain the fish, discard all skin and
bones, then flake and add to the
tomato mixture. Transfer to an
ovenproof dish.

Mash the potatoes with the
remaining butter and the milk, and
season well. Spread over the fish
mixture and fork up. Sprinkle with
the grated cheese and place in a
preheated moderately hot oven,
200°C (400°F), Gas Mark 6, for about
20 minutes or until golden on top.
**Serves 4**

# Smoked Haddock with Corn

750 g (1½ lb)
    smoked haddock
    fillets
25 g (1 oz) butter
25 g (1 oz) flour
150 ml (¼ pint)
    milk
salt and pepper
1 x 326 g (11½ oz)
    can sweetcorn,
    drained
4 tablespoons fresh
    sour cream
    (optional)
parsley sprig to
    garnish

Place the haddock in a large frying
pan and add just enough boiling
water to cover. Simmer, uncovered,
for 5 minutes, skimming the surface
occasionally. Remove the fish,
reserving 150 ml (¼ pint) of the
cooking liquor, cut into pieces and
place in a casserole.

Melt the butter in a saucepan and
stir in the flour. Cook, stirring, for 1
minute, then gradually add the milk
and reserved cooking liquor. Bring
to the boil, stirring constantly;
season well with salt and pepper.

Stir in the sweetcorn and pour the
sauce over the haddock. Cover and
cook in a preheated moderate oven,
180°C (350°F), Gas Mark 4, for 20
minutes.

Just before serving, stir in the sour
cream, if using. Garnish with parsley
and serve accompanied by boiled
potatoes or crusty bread.
**Serves 4**

# Kedgeree

500 g (1 lb) smoked
   haddock fillets
2 eggs, hard-boiled
125 g (4 oz) butter
175 g (6 oz) long-
   grain rice, cooked
1 x 198 g (7 oz) can
   pimentos, drained
   and chopped
1 tablespoon lemon
   juice
salt and pepper
2 tablespoons single
   cream or top-of-the
   milk
2 tablespoons
   chopped parsley to
   garnish

Place the haddock in a frying pan
and add just enough boiling water to
cover. Simmer for 10 to 15 minutes,
skimming the surface if necessary.
Drain and flake the fish. Cut the
hard-boiled eggs into small wedges.

Melt the butter in a pan and stir in
the rice, haddock, egg, pimento and
lemon juice. Season to taste with salt
and pepper and mix well. Cook,
stirring, over moderate heat until
heated through. Remove from the
heat and stir in the cream or
top-of-the milk. Pile into a hot
serving dish and garnish with
parsley.
**Serves 4**

# Tuna Fish Cakes

300 g (10 oz)
potatoes, boiled
25 g (1 oz) butter or
margarine
1 x 198 g (7 oz) and
1 x 99 g (3½ oz)
can tuna, drained
and flaked
2 tablespoons
chopped parsley
salt and pepper
2 eggs, beaten
75 g (3 oz) dry
breadcrumbs
oil for shallow frying
parsley sprigs to
garnish
lemon wedges to
serve

Mash the potatoes with the butter or margarine, then mix in the tuna, parsley, salt and pepper to taste and half the beaten egg.

Chill the mixture for 20 minutes, then place on a floured surface and shape into a roll. Cut into 8 slices and shape each into a flat round, about 6 cm (2½ inches) in diameter. Dip into the remaining egg, then coat with breadcrumbs.

Heat the oil in a frying pan, add the fish cakes and fry for 2 to 3 minutes on each side or until golden brown and heated through. Garnish each fish cake with a parsley sprig. Serve with lemon wedges.

**Serves 4**

# Cod with Mushrooms

4 cod steaks
175 g (6 oz)
　mushrooms, sliced
4 tomatoes, skinned
　and sliced
1 clove garlic,
　crushed (optional)
2 tablespoons white
　wine
1 tablespoon lemon
　juice
salt and pepper
chopped parsley to
　garnish

Place the cod steaks in a well greased ovenproof dish. Top with the mushrooms, tomatoes and garlic, if using. Pour over the wine and lemon juice and season well with salt and pepper.

Cover with foil and cook in a preheated moderate oven, 180°C (350°F), Gas Mark 4, for 30 minutes. Garnish with chopped parsley.
**Serves 4**

# Plaice with Spinach

750 g (1½ lb)
　spinach
3 tablespoons single
　cream
25 g (1 oz) butter,
　flaked
salt and pepper
grated nutmeg
8 small plaice fillets,
　skinned
2 tablespoons grated
　Parmesan cheese
tomato wedges to
　garnish

Cook the spinach, with just the water clinging to the leaves after washing, until tender. Drain thoroughly, then press through a sieve. Mix in the cream and butter. Season well with salt, pepper and nutmeg. Place in a greased casserole.

Roll up the plaice fillets and secure with cocktail sticks. Arrange them on the spinach and sprinkle with the cheese. Cover and cook in a preheated moderate oven, 180°C (350°F), Gas Mark 4, for 30 minutes. Garnish with tomato wedges.
**Serves 4**

# Herrings in Oatmeal

4 herrings
salt and pepper
125 g (4 oz) oatmeal
　or rolled oats
25 g (1 oz) butter
1 tablespoon oil
lemon wedges to
　serve

Cut the heads off the fish, gut them and remove the backbones. Rub the fish with a little salt. Rinse and dry, then sprinkle with salt and pepper.

Coat the fish with the oatmeal or oats, pressing firmly. Heat the butter and oil in a frying pan, add the fish and fry for about 8 minutes, turning once. Drain on kitchen paper and serve with lemon wedges.
**Serves 4**

# Layered Fish Casserole

50 g (2 oz) butter or
  margarine
4 rashers streaky
  bacon, derinded
  and chopped
2 onions, finely
  chopped
4 tomatoes, skinned
  and chopped
1 clove garlic,
  crushed (optional)
salt and pepper
1 tablespoon chopped
  parsley
4 haddock or cod
  fillets
1 tablespoon lemon
  juice
50 g (2 oz) fresh
  breadcrumbs
50 g (2 oz)
  Parmesan cheese,
  grated

Melt the butter in a frying pan. Add
the bacon, onion, tomato and garlic,
if using, and fry until the onion is
softened. Season to taste with salt
and pepper, then place in a
well-greased ovenproof dish and
sprinkle with parsley. Arrange the
fish on top and sprinkle with lemon
juice.

Mix the breadcrumbs and cheese
together and spoon evenly over the
fish. Bake in a preheated moderate
oven, 180°C (350°F), Gas Mark 4, for
30 minutes, until the fish is tender
and the topping golden brown.
**Serves 4**

# Baked Fish in Cider

1 onion, finely
  chopped
125 g (4 oz)
  mushrooms,
  chopped
4 halibut or cod
  steaks
1 egg, beaten
3 tablespoons dry
  breadcrumbs
2 teaspoons lemon
  juice
salt and pepper
4 tablespoons cider
25 g (1 oz) butter
chopped parsley to
  garnish (optional)

Place the onion and mushrooms in
an ovenproof dish.

Dip the fish steaks into the egg
and coat with breadcrumbs. Arrange
on top of the onion and mushrooms
and sprinkle with the lemon juice,
salt and pepper to taste. Spoon the
cider over the fish.

Dot with butter and bake in a
preheated moderate oven, 160°C
(325°F), Gas Mark 3, for 40 minutes
until tender. Garnish with parsley if
liked.
**Serves 4**

# MEAT & POULTRY

## Kidney Kebabs

12 lambs' kidneys
12 rashers streaky
  bacon, derinded
8 small tomatoes,
  halved
4 small onions,
  halved
50 g (2 oz) butter,
  melted

Skin, core and halve the kidneys. Cut the bacon rashers in half and roll up. Thread the ingredients alternately onto 8 skewers: kidney, tomato, bacon, onion, then repeat, finishing with bacon.

Brush with melted butter and cook under a moderately hot grill for 8 to 10 minutes, turning frequently and brushing with more butter as necessary. Serve on a bed of rice.
**Serves 4**

# Tangy Braised Beef

8 thin slices of beef
   topside
2 tablespoons made
   English mustard
flour for coating
salt and pepper
4 medium onions,
   chopped
600 ml (1 pint) beef
   stock
parsley sprig to
   garnish (optional)

Spread both sides of the beef slices with mustard. Season the flour with salt and pepper and use to coat the beef. Arrange in a casserole, top with the onion and pour over the stock.

Cover and cook in a preheated moderately hot oven, 190°C (375°F), Gas Mark 5, for 15 minutes. Lower the heat to moderate, 160°C (325°F), Gas Mark 3, and cook for 1½ to 1¾ hours, or until the meat is tender.

Garnish with parsley, if liked. Serve with vegetables of choice.
**Serves 4**

# Spaghetti Bolognaise

BOLOGNAISE SAUCE:
25 g (1 oz) butter
2 tablespoons oil
2 onions, chopped
500 g (1 lb) minced
    beef
125 g (4 oz)
    mushrooms,
    chopped
1 x 397 g (14 oz)
    can tomatoes
2 cloves garlic,
    crushed
½ teaspoon dried
    oregano
1 x 65 g (2¼ oz)
    can tomato purée
150 ml (¼ pint) beef
    stock or red wine
salt and pepper
SPAGHETTI:
250-350 g (8-12 oz)
    spaghetti
25 g (1 oz) butter
grated nutmeg
TO GARNISH:
grated Parmesan
    cheese

To make the Bolognaise sauce: Heat the butter and oil in a saucepan, add the onion and fry until softened. Add the meat and fry briskly, stirring, until evenly browned. Drain off all the excess fat, then add the remaining sauce ingredients, with salt and pepper to taste.

Bring to simmering point, stirring, then cover and simmer over low heat for 1 hour, adding more liquid if necessary.

Cook the spaghetti in boiling salted water according to packet instructions and drain thoroughly. Melt the butter in the saucepan, return the spaghetti to the pan and toss well. Season to taste with nutmeg and pepper.

Turn into a serving dish, top with the Bolognaise sauce and sprinkle with Parmesan cheese.
**Serves 4**

# Irish Stew

1 kg (2 lb) middle or
    scrag end of neck
    lamb chops, or a
    mixture of both
salt and pepper
3 large onions, sliced
1 kg (2 lb) potatoes,
    sliced
2 tablespoons
    Worcestershire
    sauce

Trim any excess fat from the lamb and arrange a layer of chops in a flameproof casserole. Sprinkle with salt and pepper. Cover with a layer of onions and then potatoes. Repeat until all onions and potatoes have been used.

Sprinkle the Worcestershire sauce over the top, then pour in enough water to come almost to the top layer of potato. Bring to the boil, cover and cook in a preheated moderate oven, 160°C (325°F), Gas Mark 3, for 2½ hours.
**Serves 4 to 6**

# Beef, Pepper and Mushroom Casserole

1 kg (2 lb) braising
    steak
3 tablespoons plain
    flour
salt and pepper
3 tablespoons oil
3 onions, chopped
1 large green pepper,
    cored, seeded and
    chopped
600 ml (1 pint) beef
    stock (or a mixture
    of stock and red
    wine)
1 bouquet garni
250 g (8 oz)
    mushrooms, sliced

Cut the meat into 2.5 (1 inch) cubes.
Season the flour with salt and pepper
and use to coat the meat.

Heat the oil in a flameproof
casserole, add the meat in batches
and quickly brown on all sides.
Remove from the casserole.

Add the onion and pepper to the
fat remaining in the casserole and fry
until softened. Return the meat to
the casserole, sprinkle in any
remaining seasoned flour and cook,
stirring, for 1 minute.

Gradually add the stock (or stock
and wine) and bring to the boil,
stirring constantly. Add the bouquet
garni, cover and cook in a preheated
moderate oven, 160°C (325°F), Gas
Mark 3, for 2 hours.

Add the mushrooms, adjust the
seasoning if necessary and cook for
30 minutes. Remove the bouquet
garni. Serve with potatoes and a
green vegetable.
**Serves 4 to 6**

# Braised Oxtail

2 oxtails, jointed
50 g (2 oz) beef
   dripping
4 medium onions,
   chopped
4 carrots, sliced
3 celery sticks,
   chopped
1 small turnip, diced
2 tablespoons plain
   flour
750 ml (1 ¼ pints)
   beef stock
salt and pepper
grated nutmeg
1 bouquet garni
1 bay leaf

Trim any excess fat from the oxtail joints. Heat the dripping in a large flameproof casserole, add the oxtail and quickly brown on all sides. Remove from the casserole.

Add the vegetables to the fat remaining in the casserole and fry until softened. Sprinkle in the flour and cook, stirring, until the flour is beginning to brown. Gradually add the stock and bring to the boil, stirring constantly.

Return the oxtail to the casserole, season well with salt, pepper and nutmeg, and add the bouquet garni and bay leaf. Cook in a preheated cool oven, 150°C (300°F), Gas Mark 2, for 4 hours, adding a little more water or stock if necessary.

Remove from the oven, allow to cool and store in the refrigerator overnight. Discard all the fat which has solidified on top of the casserole and simmer gently for 30 minutes. Remove the bouquet garni and bay leaf. Serve with creamed potatoes.
**Serves 6**

# Winter Family Casserole

1 kg (2 lb) stewing
  steak
3 tablespoons oil
25 g (1 oz) flour
750 ml (1¼ pints)
  beef stock
4 onions, chopped
250 g (8 oz) carrots,
  sliced
1 turnip, diced
salt and pepper
grated nutmeg
2 bay leaves
4 medium potatoes,
  sliced

Cut the meat into 2.5 cm (1 inch) cubes. Heat the oil in a flameproof casserole, add the meat in batches and quickly brown on all sides, moving the meat cubes to the side of the casserole as they brown.

Sprinkle in the flour and cook, stirring, for 1 minute. Gradually add the stock and bring to the boil, stirring constantly. Lower the heat to simmering point and add the onion, carrot and turnip.

Season to taste with salt, pepper and nutmeg and add the bay leaves. Cover and cook in a preheated moderate oven, 160°C (325°F), Gas Mark 3, for 1½ hours.

Add the potatoes and return to the oven for a further 1 hour. Remove the bay leaves before serving, with crusty French bread, if liked.
**Serves 4 to 6**

# Shepherds Pie

4 large potatoes,
  boiled
2 tablespoons milk
25 g (1 oz) butter
salt and pepper
500 g (1 lb) cooked
  lamb or beef
2 onions
1 clove garlic
300 ml (½ pint) beef
  stock
1 tablespoon
  Worcestershire
  sauce
½ teaspoon each
  dried thyme and
  marjoram
1 tablespoon
  cornflour blended
  with 2 tablespoons
  water

Cream the potatoes with the milk and butter and season to taste with salt and pepper.

Mince together the meat, onions and garlic. Place in a shallow flameproof dish and add the stock, Worcestershire sauce, herbs and blended cornflour. Add salt and pepper to taste and mix well. Bring to the boil, stirring, and cook, stirring, for 1 minute. Cover and simmer for 15 minutes.

Spread the potato over the meat mixture and place under a medium grill until the top is crisp and golden brown. Serve with a green vegetable.
**Serves 4**

# Liver and Tomato Casserole

25 g (1 oz) butter
1 tablespoon oil
2 onions, chopped
1 small green pepper,
    cored, seeded and
    chopped
flour for coating
salt and pepper
500 g (1 lb) pigs'
    liver
8 rashers streaky
    bacon, derinded
    and chopped
1 x 397 g (14 oz)
    can tomatoes
4 tablespoons red
    wine or water
1 tablespoon
    Worcester-
    shire sauce
chopped parsley to
    garnish (optional)

Heat the butter and oil in a
flameproof casserole, add the onion
and pepper and fry until softened.

Season the flour with salt and
pepper and use to coat the liver. Add
to the pan with the bacon. Increase
the heat slightly and continue frying,
stirring, to seal the liver. Drain off
any excess fat, then stir in the
remaining ingredients.

Cover and cook in a preheated
moderate oven, 180°C (350°F), Gas
Mark 4, for 30 minutes. Garnish
with a little chopped parsley, if liked.
**Serves 4**

# Meat Pancakes

50 g (2 oz) plain
  flour
50 g (2 oz)
  self-raising flour
1 egg
300 ml (½ pint)
  milk
salt and pepper
250 g (8 oz) cooked
  lamb, diced
1 medium onion,
  finely chopped
lard for frying
parsley sprig to
  garnish (optional)

Sift the flours into a bowl, make a well in the centre and add the egg. Add the milk a little at a time, beating thoroughly between each addition. Season well with salt and pepper. Stir in the meat and onion.

Grease an 18 cm (7 inch) non-stick frying pan with lard and place over a moderate heat. Pour in enough pancake mixture to cover the base of the pan. Cook until the underside is golden, then turn and cook the other side.

Repeat with the remaining mixture to make 6 to 8 pancakes, re-greasing the pan each time. Serve immediately, or stack them on a plate, with a piece of greaseproof paper between each one, as they cook and keep warm in the oven. Garnish with parsley, if liked.

**Serves 3 to 4**

# Lamb with Tomatoes and Mint

1 kg (2 lb) best end
    of neck lamb
    cutlets
flour for coating
25 g (1 oz) butter
2 tablespoons oil
2 onions, chopped
salt and pepper
1 x 397 g (14 oz)
    can tomatoes
150 ml (¼ pint)
    stock
1 teaspoon sugar
3 teaspoons
    concentrated mint
    sauce
mint sprig to garnish
    (optional)

Coat the cutlets with flour. Heat the
butter and oil in a flameproof
casserole. Add the meat in batches
and brown on both sides. Remove
the meat from the casserole as it
browns and keep warm. Add the
onion to the fat remaining in the
casserole and fry until softened.
Drain off any fat remaining in the
casserole.

Using a slotted spoon, return the
meat to the casserole and sprinkle
with salt and pepper to taste. Pour
the tomatoes with their juice and the
stock over the meat. Stir in the sugar
and mint sauce.

Cook in a preheated moderate
oven, 160°C (325°F), Gas Mark 3, for
1 to 1½ hours. Garnish with a mint
sprig, if liked.
**Serves 4**

# Pork 'n' Beans

1 kg (2 lb) belly of
  pork, sliced
flour for coating
salt and pepper
2 tablespoons oil
3 onions, sliced
450 ml (³/4 pint)
  stock
1 x 227 g (8 oz) can
  tomatoes
1 tablespoon vinegar
1 tablespoon soft
  brown sugar
1 teaspoon mustard
  powder
1 x 425 g (15 oz)
  can red kidney
  beans, drained

Cut the meat into cubes. Season the
flour with salt and pepper and use to
coat the meat.

Heat the oil in a flameproof
casserole, add the meat in batches
and brown on all sides. Remove the
meat as it browns and keep warm.

Add the onion to the fat in the
casserole and fry gently until turning
golden. Drain off any excess fat and
return the meat to the casserole.

Add the stock, tomatoes and their
juice, vinegar, sugar and mustard and
bring to the boil, stirring. Cover and
cook in a preheated moderate oven,
160°C (325°F), Gas Mark 3, for 2
hours.

Stir in the kidney beans, check the
seasoning and cook for a further 30
minutes to 1 hour or until tender.
**Serves 4 to 6**

# Cidered Pork

50 g (2 oz) lard
750 g (1½ lb) boned
  shoulder of pork,
  cubed
salt and pepper
250 g (8 oz) streaky
  bacon, derinded
  and chopped
500 g (1 lb) cooking
  apples, peeled,
  cored and sliced
500 g (1 lb) onions,
  sliced
4 large potatoes,
  thickly sliced
150 ml (¼ pint)
  cider
150-300 ml (¼-½
  pint) stock
25 g (1 oz) butter

Melt the lard in a frying pan, add the
pork and brown on all sides.
Remove from the pan and drain off
excess fat. Place in a casserole and
season well with salt and pepper.

Add the bacon to the fat remaining
in the pan, fry lightly then transfer to
the casserole with a slotted spoon.

Arrange the apple and onion over
the meat, then top with the potato.
Pour in the cider and just enough
stock to come up to the potato.
Sprinkle with salt and pepper, cover
and cook in a preheated moderate
oven, 180°C (350°F), Gas Mark 4, for
1 hour.

Remove the lid and dot the potato
with butter. Increase the heat to
moderately hot, 200°C (400°F), Gas
Mark 6, and cook, uncovered, for 30
minutes, or until golden brown.
**Serves 4**

# Honey-Baked Gammon

1.25 kg (2½ lb)
    piece middle or
    corner gammon
125 g (4 oz) honey
1 teaspoon made
    mustard
½ teaspoon ground
    cloves
150 ml (¼ pint)
    cider or stock

Cover the gammon with cold water and leave to soak for 2 hours. Drain, place in a large saucepan and cover with fresh cold water. Bring to the boil, skim, cover and simmer gently for 35 minutes. Drain again and cut off the rind.

Place the gammon in a roasting pan. Mix together the honey, mustard and cloves and spread over the gammon. Pour the cider or stock into the pan and bake in a preheated moderately hot oven, 200°C (400°F), Gas Mark 6, for 35 to 40 minutes, basting frequently.

Transfer the gammon to a serving plate. Pour any liquid remaining in the pan into a sauceboat and hand separately. Serve with peas and potatoes.

**Serves 6 to 8**

# Southern-Fried Chicken

*flour for coating*
*salt and pepper*
*1-1½ teaspoons*
*grated nutmeg*
*4 chicken pieces*
*5 tablespoons milk*
*oil for shallow frying*
*parsley sprig to*
*garnish*

Season the flour with a little salt, a generous amount of pepper and the nutmeg. Dip the chicken pieces into the milk, then coat thoroughly with flour. Dip into the milk again, then coat again with flour.

Pour oil into a deep frying pan to a depth of about 2.5 cm (1 inch). Heat the oil, then add the chicken pieces and fry for 20 minutes, turning once. Drain well. Garnish with parsley and serve hot or cold with a salad.
**Serves 4**

# Chicken Pie

50 g (2 oz) butter
40 g (1½ oz) plain flour
150 ml (¼ pint) milk
300 ml (½ pint) chicken stock
350 g (12 oz) cooked chicken, diced
125 g (4 oz) mushrooms, chopped
½ green pepper, cored, seeded and chopped
1 tablespoon chopped parsley
½ teaspoon celery salt
salt and pepper
1 x 212 g (7½ oz) packet frozen puff pastry, thawed
beaten egg to glaze

Melt the butter in a saucepan and stir in the flour. Cook, stirring, for 1 minute. Gradually add the milk and stock and bring to the boil, stirring constantly. Stir in the chicken, mushrooms, green pepper and parsley. Season with the celery salt and salt and pepper to taste. Transfer to a 1.2 litre (2 pint) pie dish. Place a pie funnel in the middle.

Roll out the pastry to 2.5 cm (1 inch) larger than the dish. Cut off a 1 cm (½ inch) strip all round and place on the dampened edge of the dish. Moisten the strip with water, then cover with the pastry lid, pressing down firmly. Trim and flute the edge. Decorate with pastry leaves made from the trimmings, if liked, then brush with beaten egg.

Bake near the top of a preheated hot oven, 220°C (425°F), Gas Mark 7, for 30 minutes until golden.
**Serves 4 to 6**

# Orange-Baked Chicken

2 large oranges
50 g (2 oz) butter
1 tablespoon oil
4 chicken pieces
2 onions, finely
    chopped
2 tablespoons
    Worcestershire
    sauce
2 tablespoons water
1 tablespoon tomato
    purée
salt and pepper

Thinly pare the rind from 1 orange, and cut the rind into thin strips. Grate the rind from the other orange, and squeeze the juice from both.

Heat the butter and oil in a frying pan, add the chicken pieces and brown on both sides. Remove from the pan and keep warm. Add the onion to the fat remaining in the pan and fry gently for 5 minutes.

Drain off any fat, then add the Worcestershire sauce, water, tomato purée, orange rind (strips and grated) and juice. Bring to the boil and season lightly with salt and pepper.

Line a shallow ovenproof dish or roasting pan with foil, leaving enough on either side to overlap in the middle. Place the chicken on the foil, spoon over the orange sauce, then cover with the foil, securing the edges by folding together. Bake in a preheated moderate oven, 180°C (350°F), Gas Mark 4, for 1 hour.

To serve, spoon the juices over the chicken. Serve with jacket potatoes.
**Serves 4**

# Mustard-Glazed Chicken

4 chicken pieces
2 tablespoons Dijon
    mustard
2 tablespoons made
    English mustard
50 g (2 oz) caster
    sugar
4 tablespoons lemon
    juice
2 tablespoons oil
1-2 teaspoons
    Worcestershire
    sauce
salt and pepper

Arrange the chicken pieces, skin side down, on a grill pan. Put the remaining ingredients, with salt and pepper to taste, in a bowl. Beat well.

Spoon about one quarter of the glaze over the chicken and cook under a moderate grill for 15 minutes, spooning over more glaze halfway through cooking. Turn the chicken pieces over, glaze the skin side with more mustard mixture and cook for 15 to 30 minutes until tender, spooning over the remaining glaze during cooking.

Serve with lettuce.
**Serves 4**

# Chicken and Sultana Casserole

*50 g (2 oz) plain
    flour*
*salt and pepper*
*grated nutmeg*
*4 chicken pieces*
*50 g (2 oz) butter*
*2 tablespoons oil*
*2 onions, chopped*
*4 rashers streaky
    bacon, derinded
    and chopped*
*600 ml (1 pint)
    chicken stock*
*250 g (8 oz)
    mushrooms, sliced*
*4 tomatoes, skinned
    and chopped*
*125 g (4 oz)
    sultanas*

Season the flour with salt, pepper and nutmeg to taste and use to coat the chicken pieces.

Heat the butter and oil in a flameproof casserole, add the chicken and fry, turning frequently, for about 10 minutes or until golden brown all over. Remove from the casserole and keep warm.

Add the onion and bacon to the fat remaining in the casserole and fry until the onion is softened. Sprinkle in any remaining seasoned flour and cook, stirring, for 1 minute. Gradually add the stock and bring to the boil, stirring.

Return the chicken to the casserole and add the mushrooms, tomatoes and sultanas. Cover and cook in a preheated moderate oven, 180°C (350°F), Gas Mark 4, for 1 hour or until tender.
**Serves 4**

## Courgettes with Tomatoes

50 g (2 oz) butter or
  margarine
2 tablespoons olive or
  cooking oil
4 large courgettes,
  sliced
4 large tomatoes,
  chopped
2 cloves garlic,
  crushed (optional)
salt and pepper

Heat the butter or margarine and oil in a large frying pan and fry the courgette slices on one side until golden brown. Turn them over and add the tomatoes to the pan just as the courgettes are beginning to brown on the second side. Mix well, add the garlic, if using, season to taste with salt and pepper and continue cooking until the tomatoes are tender. This dish is delicious served with plain grilled meat.
**Serves 4**

# Glazed Carrots

500 g (1 lb) carrots
salt
1 chicken or beef
    stock cube
1 tablespoon sugar
50 g (2 oz) butter or
    margarine
chopped parsley to
    garnish (optional)

Leave the carrots whole if small and tender, otherwise slice into rings. Put in a saucepan with just enough lightly salted water to come up to the level of the carrots. Bring to the boil and add the remaining ingredients. Cover and cook for about 20 minutes, then remove the lid and continue cooking for a further 10 to 15 minutes or until the carrots are cooked and the water has nearly boiled away. Drain and serve sprinkled with parsley if liked.
**Serves 4**

# Savoury Cauliflower Cheese

1 cauliflower, broken
    into florets
salt and pepper
75 g (3 oz) butter
2 onions, chopped
4 rashers streaky
    bacon, derinded
    and chopped
25 g (1 oz) plain
    flour
300 ml (½ pint)
    milk
125 g (4 oz)
    Cheddar cheese,
    grated
1 tablespoon oil
125 g (4 oz)
    mushrooms,
    chopped

Cook the cauliflower in boiling
salted water for 10 to 15 minutes
until tender. Drain thoroughly.

Melt half the butter in a saucepan,
add the onion and bacon and fry
gently for 5 minutes. Stir in the flour
and cook, stirring, for 1 minute.
Gradually stir in the milk and bring
to the boil, stirring. Cook, stirring,
for 2 minutes. Remove from the heat
and add all but 1 tablespoon of the
cheese.

Meanwhile, heat the remaining
butter and the oil in a frying pan, add
the mushrooms and fry over fairly
high heat. Remove from the pan
with a slotted spoon, and stir into the
cheese sauce. Season with salt and
pepper to taste.

Arrange the cauliflower in a
warmed ovenproof dish and pour the
sauce over the top. Sprinkle with the
reserved cheese and place under a
preheated grill until golden.
**Serves 4**

# Stuffed Marrow

1 x 1 kg (2 lb)
  marrow
1 tablespoon oil
50 g (2 oz) butter
1 onion, finely
  chopped
125 g (4 oz) streaky
  bacon, derinded
  and finely chopped
1 clove garlic,
  crushed (optional)
250 g (8 oz) minced
  beef
4 tablespoons fresh
  breadcrumbs
2 tomatoes, skinned
  and chopped
½ teaspoon mixed
  dried herbs
salt and pepper
grated nutmeg

Peel the marrow, cut the flesh into
5 cm (2 inch) rounds and remove the
seeds. Place upright in a well greased
large ovenproof dish.

Heat the oil and half the butter in a
frying pan, add the onion, bacon and
garlic, if using, and fry gently until
softened. Add the beef, increase the
heat and fry briskly until brown.
Drain off any excess fat, then mix in
the breadcrumbs, tomatoes and
herbs. Season well with salt and
pepper.

Sprinkle the marrow rings with
salt, pepper and nutmeg, then fill
with the stuffing. Dot with the
remaining butter, cover with foil and
bake in a preheated moderate oven,
180°C (350°F), Gas Mark 4, for 35 to
45 minutes or until the rings are
tender. Serve with crusty French
bread.
**Serves 4**

# Potatoes with Onions

6 tablespoons beef
   dripping jelly, or
   2 beef stock cubes
4 medium onions,
   thinly sliced into
   rings
salt and pepper
4-6 medium potatoes,
   cut into 5 mm
   (¼ inch) slices

If using beef dripping jelly, place in a small roasting pan and melt down with enough boiling water to cover the bottom of the pan to a depth of about 2.5 cm (1 inch). Alternatively crumble the beef stock cubes into the pan and add the water as above.

Arrange the onion rings in the bottom of the pan and sprinkle with pepper and a little salt.

Arrange the potato slices on top, season again, cover with foil and simmer over a low heat for 20 to 30 minutes until the vegetables are tender.

This Australian dish is delicious served as a snack with crusty bread, or as an accompaniment to roast beef.
**Serves 4**

# Creamed Cauliflower

1 medium
   cauliflower,
   broken into florets
salt and pepper
25 g (1 oz) butter
25 g (1 oz) flour
300 ml (½ pint)
   milk
grated nutmeg

Cook the cauliflower in lightly salted boiling water for about 10 to 15 minutes, or until tender. Drain well.

Meanwhile, melt the butter in a small pan and stir in the flour. Cook, stirring, for 1 minute, then gradually stir in the milk. Bring to the boil, stirring constantly, then season to taste with salt, pepper and nutmeg. Cook, stirring, for 2 minutes.

Return the cauliflower to the saucepan and mash down with a potato masher or a wooden spoon. Pour in the white sauce and beat into the cauliflower until smooth. Pile into a vegetable dish and sprinkle with a little more nutmeg.
**Serves 4**

# Buttered Leeks with Nutmeg

*6-8 leeks, sliced*
*salt and pepper*
*50 g (2 oz) butter*
*grated nutmeg*

Cook the leeks in a pan of boiling salted water for 10 minutes. Drain well. Melt the butter in the saucepan and return the leeks to the pan. Toss well and sprinkle with plenty of nutmeg and freshly ground pepper.
**Serves 4**

49

# Swede with Bacon

1 medium swede, cut
   into 2.5 cm
   (1 inch) cubes
salt and pepper
4 rashers streaky
   bacon, derinded
   and chopped
grated nutmeg
2 tablespoons milk or
   single cream

Cook the swede in boiling salted
water for about 30 minutes or until
tender. Drain thoroughly.

Meanwhile, fry the bacon in its
own fat until crisp.

Return the swede to the saucepan,
add the fat from the bacon and mash
to a pulp. Stir in the bacon and
season with plenty of freshly ground
pepper and nutmeg. Stir in the milk
or cream and heat through. This dish
is delicious with roast pork.
**Serves 4**

# Potato Cakes

2 eggs, beaten
salt and pepper
2 tablespoons
  chopped parsley
4 medium potatoes,
  grated
1 small onion, grated
  (optional)
50 g (2 oz) Cheddar
  cheese, grated
  (optional)
oil for shallow frying

Season the beaten egg with plenty of salt and freshly ground pepper and add the parsley. Drain any liquid from the potato and stir into the egg mixture. Add the onion and cheese, if using.

Heat a little oil in a frying pan, then place about 2 tablespoons of the potato mixture in the pan. Flatten slightly to form a pancake shape, then cover the pan and cook gently for about 4 minutes on each side, or until golden brown.

Transfer to a serving dish and keep hot. Repeat with the remaining mixture. Serve with tomato ketchup.
**Makes 6 to 8**

# Grape and Orange Salad with Ham

2 large oranges
1 crisp lettuce
½ cucumber, peeled
and diced
1 green pepper,
cored, seeded and
chopped
250 g (8 oz) seedless
grapes
4 slices of ham
150 ml (¼ pint)
French Dressing
(see page 57)

Using a serrated knife, peel the oranges, removing all the pith. Cut each segment into 3 or 4 pieces.

Line a salad bowl with a layer of lettuce leaves and arrange a layer of orange, cucumber, pepper and grapes on top. Repeat the layers until all these ingredients are used up.

Roll up the ham slices and arrange on top of the salad. Serve French dressing separately.
**Serves 4**

# Cabbage, Carrot and Apple Salad

2 crisp eating apples
juice of 1 lemon
½ white cabbage,
shredded
250 g (8 oz) carrots,
shredded
½ teaspoon dried
oregano
150 ml (¼ pint)
French dressing
(see page 57)

Peel and thinly slice the apples and coat thoroughly with the lemon juice. Place in a salad bowl with the cabbage and carrot and mix well.

Add the oregano to the French dressing, pour over the salad and toss thoroughly.
**Serves 4**

# Tomato and Cucumber Salad

6-8 tomatoes, sliced
½-1 cucumber,
peeled and thinly
sliced
salt and pepper
1 teaspoon caster
sugar
150 ml (¼ pint)
French dressing
(see page 57)
½ teaspoon dried
marjoram

Arrange the tomato and cucumber slices in a shallow serving dish and sprinkle with salt and pepper to taste and the sugar. Leave to stand for at least 10 minutes.

Pour over the French dressing and sprinkle with the marjoram. Serve immediately. This salad makes a delicious side dish to grilled meats and pasta dishes.
**Serves 4**

# Warm Potato Salad

4 medium potatoes,
cooked
3 eggs, hard-boiled
2 medium onions,
chopped
1 small green pepper,
cored, seeded and
finely chopped
1-2 tablespoons
snipped chives
1 tablespoon chopped
parsley
1½ tablespoons cider
vinegar or lemon
juice
1 clove garlic,
crushed (optional)
1 teaspoon
horseradish sauce
freshly ground black
pepper

Dice the potatoes and eggs while still
warm. Place in a serving bowl and
add the remaining ingredients, with
pepper to taste. Toss lightly.

Serve immediately, with
mayonnaise, as an accompaniment to
cold beef, pork or ham.

**Serves 4**

# Rice Salad

175 g (6 oz)
  long-grain rice,
  cooked
1 green pepper,
  cored, seeded and
  chopped
250 g (8 oz)
  tomatoes, skinned
  and chopped
1 x 326 g (11½ oz)
  can sweetcorn,
  drained
2 tablespoons
  sultanas
1 small onion, finely
  chopped
2 sticks celery, finely
  chopped
2 tablespoons
  chopped parsley
French dressing (see
  page 57)
salt and pepper

Mix together the rice, pepper, tomatoes, sweetcorn, sultanas, onion, celery and parsley in a large bowl. Add enough French dressing to moisten the mixture and season to taste with salt and pepper. Serve with cold chicken or ham.

**Serves 4**

# Cauliflower, Mushroom and Onion Salad

125 g (4 oz) button
   mushrooms, thinly
   sliced
juice of 1 lemon
1 small cauliflower,
   broken into florets
2 onions, finely
   chopped
salt and pepper
1-2 tablespoons olive
   oil
150 ml (¼ pint)
   French dressing
   (see page 57)
paprika to garnish

Sprinkle the mushrooms with the
lemon juice and put into a salad bowl
with the cauliflower and onion.
Season to taste with salt and pepper.

   Add the olive oil to the French
dressing and pour over the
vegetables. Leave to marinate for 30
minutes, stirring occasionally.

   Just before serving, sprinkle with
paprika. This salad is delicious with
fish.

**Serves 4**

# French Dressing

14 tablespoons olive or
corn oil
6 tablespoons wine
vinegar, or 4
tablespoons wine
vinegar and 2
tablespoons lemon
juice
3/4 teaspoon salt
freshly ground black
pepper to taste
1 1/2 teaspoons caster
sugar
2 cloves garlic,
crushed, or a little
garlic salt
1 teaspoon made
mustard (Dijon, if
possible)

Place all the ingredients in a bowl
and beat together thoroughly with a
hand whisk or electric mixer.
Alternatively place the ingredients in
a screw-top jar and shake vigorously.
Always give a final mix immediately
before serving.
**Makes approximately 300 ml
(1/2 pint)**

# SUPPERS & SNACKS

## Tomato and Cheese Savouries

4 pieces pitta bread
1 x 65 g (2¼ oz)
    can tomato purée
500 g (1 lb)
    tomatoes, thinly
    sliced
125 g (4 oz)
    mushrooms, thinly
    sliced
½-1 teaspoon garlic
    salt
½-1 teaspoon dried
    marjoram
½-1 teaspoon dried
    basil
salt and pepper
125 g (4 oz)
    Cheddar cheese,
    grated

Spread the bread thinly with tomato purée, then cover with tomato and mushroom slices. Sprinkle with the garlic salt, herbs and salt and pepper to taste. Top with the grated cheese.

Place on a greased baking sheet and bake in a preheated moderately hot oven, 200°C (400°F), Gas Mark 6, for 15 minutes, or until the cheese has melted and the bread is heated through.

**Serves 4**

# Hamburgers

500 g (1 lb) minced
  beef
1 small onion,
  minced or grated
1 egg, beaten
½ teaspoon dried
  mixed herbs
1 teaspoon
  Worcestershire
  sauce
salt and pepper
50 g (2 oz) butter
2 tomatoes, sliced
4-8 soft rolls

Place the beef in a bowl and mix in
the onion, egg, herbs, Worcestershire
sauce and salt and pepper to taste.
Stir well to bind the mixture, then
shape into 4 to 8 flat round cakes.

Melt the butter in a frying pan,
add the hamburgers and fry for
about 4 to 8 minutes, depending on
size, turning once.

Meanwhile, grill the tomato slices.
Top each hamburger with a slice of
tomato and place in a soft roll. Serve
with salad and chips.

**Makes 4 to 8**

# Onion, Cheese and Egg Bake

4 onions, chopped
salt and pepper
1 green pepper,
    cored, seeded and
    chopped
300 g (10 oz)
    Cheddar cheese,
    grated
6 eggs
6 tablespoons milk
2 tablespoons
    Worcestershire
    sauce

Cook the onion in lightly salted boiling water for 5 minutes. Drain, then place half in an ovenproof dish. Sprinkle with half the chopped pepper, then half the cheese. Repeat the layers.

Beat the remaining ingredients together, with salt and pepper to taste, pour into the dish and cook in a preheated moderate oven, 180°C (350°F), Gas Mark 4, for 30 minutes. Serve with crusty bread.

**Serves 4**

# Savoury Leek Flan

PASTRY:
175 g (6 oz) plain
    flour
1/2 teaspoon salt
40 g (1 1/2 oz)
    margarine
40 g (1 1/2 oz) lard
1-2 tablespoons
    water
FILLING:
500 g (1 lb) leeks,
    sliced
25 g (1 oz) butter
25 g (1 oz) plain
    flour
300 ml (1/2 pint)
    milk
1/2 teaspoon made
    mustard
salt and pepper
175 g (6 oz) salami
    or garlic sausage,
    sliced
50 g (2 oz) Cheddar
    cheese, grated

Sift the flour and salt into a bowl. Rub in the fat until the mixture resembles breadcrumbs. Stir in enough water to bind the mixture together. Knead gently until smooth. Cover and chill for 30 minutes.

Roll out and use to line a 20 cm (8 inch) metal flan tin. Prick the base all over and bake blind in a preheated moderately hot oven, 200°C (400°F), Gas Mark 6, for 10 minutes.

Meanwhile, prepare the filling. Cook the leeks in boiling salted water for about 7 minutes. Drain, cool, then place in the flan case.

Melt the butter in a small pan, add the flour and cook, stirring, for 1 minute. Remove from the heat and gradually stir in the milk. Bring to the boil, stirring, then simmer for 2 minutes until thick and smooth. Add the mustard and salt and pepper to taste. Cool slightly, then pour over the leeks. Arrange the salami or garlic sausage on top and sprinkle with the cheese.

Return to the oven for about 15 minutes until the cheese is melted. Serve hot or cold with salad.

**Serves 4 to 6**

# Quick Ham Pizza

DOUGH:
*125 g (4 oz)*
  *self-raising flour*
*½ teaspoon baking*
  *powder*
*½ teaspoon made*
  *mustard*
*¼ teaspoon salt*
*25 g (1 oz) Cheddar*
  *cheese, grated*
*½ teaspoon paprika*
*25 g (1 oz) butter*
*1 egg, beaten*
*1 tablespoon milk*
TOPPING:
*50 g (2 oz) butter*
*1 large onion,*
  *chopped*
*1 small green pepper,*
  *cored, seeded and*
  *chopped*
*175 g (6 oz) ham*
*50 g (2 oz) garlic*
  *sausage*

Mix together all the dough
ingredients then knead lightly on a
floured board. Roll out to a 23 cm
(9 inch) round and place on a well
greased baking sheet. Either fold up
the edges of the dough to make a
rim, or put a flan ring around the
outside of the pizza. Chill while
preparing the topping.

Melt the butter in a frying pan,
add the onion and pepper and fry
until the onion begins to brown. Cut
the ham and garlic sausage into thin
strips and mix with the onion and
pepper. Spread over the pizza base.
Bake in a preheated moderately hot
oven, 200°C (400°F), Gas Mark 6, for
30 minutes. Serve immediately.
**Makes one 23 cm (9 inch) pizza**

# Savoury Quiche

PASTRY:
*175 g (6 oz) plain flour*
*½ teaspoon salt*
*40 g (1½ oz) margarine*
*40 g (1½ oz) lard*
*1-2 tablespoons water*

FILLING:
*25 g (1 oz) butter*
*4 rashers streaky bacon, derinded and chopped*
*1 small onion, sliced*
*50 g (2 oz) Cheddar cheese, grated*
*2 eggs, beaten*
*150 ml (¼ pint) milk*
*salt and pepper*

Prepare and bake the pastry case as for Savoury Leek Flan (see page 60).

Melt the butter in a frying pan, add the bacon and onion and fry until golden. Place in the prepared flan case.

Mix together the cheese, eggs, milk and salt and pepper to taste and pour over the bacon and onion. Return to the oven for 25 to 30 minutes or until set. Serve hot or cold.

**Serves 4 to 6**

# Traditional Pizza Napolitana

DOUGH:
250 g (8 oz) plain
   flour
1 teaspoon salt
15 g (1/2 oz) fresh
   yeast
150 ml (1/4 pint)
   lukewarm milk
1 egg, beaten
40 g (1 1/2 oz) butter,
   softened

TOPPING:
2 tablespoons oil
1 onion, chopped
350 g (12 oz)
   tomatoes, skinned
   and chopped
2 tablespoons water
1 x 65 g (2 1/4 oz)
   can tomato purée
1 teaspoon sugar
salt and pepper
1 clove garlic, crushed
1 bay leaf
1 teaspoon dried
   oregano
125 g (4 oz)
   Mozzarella or Bel
   Paese cheese, sliced
1 x 49 g (1 3/4 oz)
   can anchovy fillets
20 black olives

Sift the flour and salt into a mixing bowl and make a well in the centre. Cream the yeast with a little of the milk and pour into the well. Add the remaining milk and the egg and beat into the flour. Mix in the butter.

Work the dough with your hand until it leaves the sides of the bowl clean, cover with a piece of oiled plastic wrap and leave in a warm place for about 40 minutes until doubled in size.

Meanwhile, make the topping. Heat the oil in a frying pan, add the onion and fry until soft. Add the tomatoes, water, tomato purée, sugar, salt and pepper to taste, garlic, bay leaf and oregano. Simmer for 10 to 15 minutes or until the mixture is thick. Cool and remove the bay leaf.

Transfer the dough to a greased and floured baking sheet and pat out to a 23 cm (9 inch) round. Spread with the topping to within 2 cm (3/4 inch) of the edge. Cover with the cheese slices, then arrange the anchovy fillets and olives on top.

Leave to rise in a warm place for 15 minutes, then bake in a preheated hot oven, 220°C (425°F), Gas Mark 7, for 20 to 25 minutes. Serve hot.
**Makes one 23 cm (9 inch) pizza**

# Potatoes with Cheese

½ teaspoon garlic
  salt
750 g (1½ lb)
  potatoes, sliced
salt and pepper
grated nutmeg
250 g (8 oz)
  Cheddar cheese,
  grated
300 ml (½ pint)
  milk

Butter an ovenproof dish and
sprinkle with garlic salt. Arrange a
third of the potato in the dish and
season to taste with salt, pepper and
nutmeg. Cover with a third of the
cheese. Repeat the layers until the
potatoes and cheese have been used
up, then pour the milk over the top.

Cook in a preheated moderate
oven, 180°C (350°F), Gas Mark 4, for
1 hour or until tender. Serve with
French bread.
**Serves 6**

# DESSERTS

## Family Fruit Salad

juice and grated rind
of 1 lemon
2 red-skinned apples
2 bananas, peeled
1 x 212 g (7½ oz)
can peach slices
1 x 227 g (8 oz) can
pineapple pieces
2 oranges

Pour the lemon juice into a glass serving dish. Core and slice the apples, slice the bananas, and add both to the dish. Add the peaches and pineapple with their syrup. Remove all the skin and pith from the oranges, cut into slices, and add to the fruit salad with any juice. Mix the fruits together thoroughly and sprinkle with the lemon rind. Chill for at least 1 hour before serving.
**Serves 6**

# Banana Splits

4 bananas
juice of ½ lemon
1 x 75 g (3 oz) bar
   milk chocolate,
   coarsely grated
TOPPING:
whipped cream or ice
   cream
chopped walnuts
   (optional)

Peel the bananas and split lengthwise without cutting right through. Sprinkle with lemon juice. Spoon the grated chocolate into the banana splits. Wrap each banana separately in foil and place on a baking sheet.

Cook in a preheated moderate oven, 180°C (350°F), Gas Mark 4, for 20 minutes. Unwrap and serve topped with cream or ice cream and chopped walnuts, if liked.
**Serves 4**

# Layered Fruit Jelly

1 x 227 g (8 oz) can
    pineapple pieces
1 lemon jelly
2 bananas
juice of 1 lemon
125 g (4 oz)
    raspberries
125 g (4 oz)
    cherries, stoned

Drain the pineapple, reserving the syrup. Add water to the syrup to make the amount of liquid required for the jelly, then make up the jelly, following packet instructions.

Slice the bananas and sprinkle with the lemon juice. Set aside with the pineapple, raspberries and cherries.

Pour about 2.5 cm (1 inch) of the jelly into a dampened mould (or individual moulds) and arrange the bananas in the jelly. Allow to set, then add another layer of jelly and arrange another layer of fruit in this.

Repeat the layers until all the ingredients are used up, being sure to allow the jelly to set each time. When the jelly is completely set, turn out onto a plate to serve.

**Serves 6**

# Fluffy Orange Pudding

juice and grated rind
    of 1 orange
50 g (2 oz) soft
    margarine
125 g (4 oz) caster
    sugar
300 ml (½ pint)
    milk
50 g (2 oz)
    self-raising flour
2 eggs, separated

Put all the ingredients, except the egg whites, into an electric blender and blend until smooth. Alternatively, put the orange juice and rind, margarine and sugar in a bowl and beat until light and fluffy, then gradually stir in the milk. Beat in the flour and egg yolks. Whisk the egg whites until stiff, then fold into the mixture.

Turn into a greased 1 litre (1¾ pint) ovenproof dish and place in a roasting pan containing enough water to come halfway up the sides of the dish.

Cook in a preheated moderately hot oven, 190°C (375°F), Gas Mark 5, for 50 minutes.

**Serves 4**

# Raspberry Fool

2 x 212 g (7½ oz)
   cans raspberries
150 ml (¼ pint)
   custard, cooled
170 ml (6 fl oz)
   double cream,
   whipped
sponge fingers to
   serve

Drain the raspberries, reserving the syrup and a few raspberries for decoration. Purée the rest by rubbing through a sieve or working in an electric blender, adding a little of the syrup if necessary. Fold in the custard and cream.

Pour into 4 glass serving dishes and top with the reserved raspberries. Chill before serving, with sponge fingers.

**Serves 4**

69

# Baked Apples

4 medium cooking
  apples
1 teaspoon ground
  cinnamon
25 g (1 oz) butter
25 g (1 oz) icing
  sugar, sifted
1 egg yolk
50 g (2 oz) ground
  almonds
grated rind of 1
  orange
25 g (1 oz) demerara
  sugar
4 tablespoons water

Core the apples, then make a cut in the skin around the middle. Stand them in an ovenproof dish and sprinkle cinnamon around the inside of the core cavities.

Cream together the butter, icing sugar, egg yolk, almonds and orange rind and spoon into the apples. Top with demerara sugar.

Pour the water into the dish, then bake in a preheated moderate oven, 180°C (350°F), Gas Mark 4, for 45 minutes to 1 hour, until the apples are tender.

**Serves 4**

# Queen Pudding

75 g (3 oz) white
  bread, crusts
  removed
450 ml (³/4 pint)
  milk
40 g (1½ oz) butter
2 eggs, separated
75 g (3 oz) caster
  sugar
grated rind of 1
  lemon
3 tablespoons jam

Cut the bread into small cubes or grate coarsely and place in a greased 1.2 litre (2 pint) ovenproof dish.

Heat the milk and butter until just warm. Beat the egg yolks with half the sugar. Add the lemon rind and pour on the warmed milk, stirring well. Pour this custard over the bread and bake in a preheated moderate oven, 180°C (350°F), Gas Mark 4, for 25 minutes or until set.

Warm the jam and spread it over the pudding. Whisk the egg whites until stiff and fold in the remaining sugar. Pile the meringue on top of the jam and return to the oven for a further 10 to 15 minutes until the meringue is crisp.

**Serves 4**

# Rhubarb and Apple Cobbler

500 g (1 lb) rhubarb,
  chopped
500 g (1 lb) cooking
  apples, peeled,
  cored and sliced
125 g (4 oz) caster
  sugar
1 teaspoon ground
  cinnamon
175 g (6 oz)
  self-raising flour
50 g (2 oz) butter or
  margarine
120 ml (4 fl oz)
  milk
  (approximately)

Put the prepared fruit in a saucepan with just enough water to cover the bottom of the pan. Add half the sugar and simmer for about 15 minutes until tender. Stir in the cinnamon and transfer to an ovenproof dish.

Sift the flour into a mixing bowl and rub in the fat until the mixture resembles breadcrumbs. Add the remaining sugar then stir in enough milk, a little at a time, to give a fairly soft dough.

Turn onto a lightly floured board and pat out to a 1 cm (½ inch) thickness. Cut into 3.5 cm (1½ inch) rounds, using a biscuit cutter, and arrange over the fruit.

Brush with a little milk and bake in a preheated moderately hot oven, 200°C (400°F), Gas Mark 6, for 15 to 20 minutes, or until the topping is golden.
**Serves 4**

# Peach and Rice Meringue

1 x 439 g (15½ oz)
can creamed rice
pudding
4 fresh peaches,
skinned and sliced,
or 1 x 411 g
(14½ oz) can
peach slices,
drained
4 tablespoons
redcurrant jelly
juice of ½ lemon
2 egg whites
75 g (3 oz) caster
sugar

Pour the rice into an ovenproof dish
and arrange the peach slices on top.
Gently warm the redcurrant jelly
with the lemon juice, then pour over
the peaches.

Whisk the egg whites until stiff,
whisk in half the caster sugar, then
fold in the rest. Spoon the meringue
over the fruit and place in a
preheated moderate oven, 180°C
(350°F), Gas Mark 4, for 15 to 20
minutes until golden.

**Serves 6**

# Ginger Layer Dessert

3 x 212 g (7½ oz)
    cans peach slices,
    mandarins or pear
    quarters, or a
    mixture of these
1 x 200 g (7 oz)
    packet gingernuts,
    broken into pieces
284 ml (10 fl oz)
    double cream,
    lightly whipped
chocolate vermicelli
    to decorate

Drain the cans of fruit, reserving the syrup. Place one third of the gingernuts in a layer in the bottom of a 1.2 litre (2 pint) soufflé dish and spoon over just enough of the fruit syrup to moisten the biscuits. Arrange one third of the fruit on top and cover with a layer of cream.

Repeat the layers twice and chill in the refrigerator for a few hours. Decorate with chocolate vermicelli before serving.

**Serves 4 to 6**

# Pears with Chocolate Sauce

8 peeled fresh, or
    canned pear halves
125 g (4 oz) plain
    chocolate, chopped
15 g (½ oz) butter
2 tablespoons golden
    syrup
2 tablespoons milk
TOPPING:
whipped cream
chopped walnuts
    (optional)

Arrange the pear halves in 4 individual serving dishes. Place the chocolate in a basin over a pan of boiling water and add the butter and syrup. When melted, stir in the milk. Pour the sauce over the pears, allow to cool, then top with cream. Sprinkle with chopped walnuts, if liked.

**Serves 4**

# Ginger Gooseberry Pudding

2 x 283 g (10 oz)
    cans gooseberries
2 teaspoons ground
    ginger
75 g (3 oz) soft
    margarine
75 g (3 oz) caster
    sugar
1 egg, beaten
125 g (4 oz)
    self-raising flour
1-2 tablespoons milk

Drain the gooseberries, reserving the syrup. Place the gooseberries in a greased ovenproof dish, pour 2 tablespoons of the syrup over them and sprinkle with half the ginger.

Place the margarine, sugar, egg, flour, milk and remaining ginger in a bowl and beat for 2 to 3 minutes until smooth. Spoon over the fruit.

Bake in a preheated moderate oven, 180°C (350°F), Gas Mark 4, for 40 to 45 minutes.

Warm the remaining syrup and serve with the pudding.

**Serves 4**

# Bread Pudding

1 large white loaf
75 g (3 oz) shredded
suet
350 g (12 oz) mixed
dried fruit
50 g (2 oz) mixed
peel
2 tablespoons
mixed spice
1 tablespoon golden
syrup
75 g (3 oz)
margarine
125 g (4 oz) soft
brown sugar
2 eggs, beaten
2 tablespoons
demerara sugar

Slice the loaf, place in a large bowl and add just enough water to cover. Leave to soak for 30 minutes, then place in a colander and press out any excess water.

Transfer the bread to a mixing bowl and beat until smooth. Stir in the suet, fruit, peel, spice and syrup.

Cream together the margarine and soft brown sugar, then beat in the eggs. Add to the bread and mix well.

Turn into a greased ovenproof dish and sprinkle with the demerara sugar. Bake in a preheated moderately hot oven, 190°C (375°F), Gas Mark 5, for 1¼ to 1½ hours until firm and golden. Serve hot, with custard or cream.
**Serves 6**

# Apple and Date Steamed Pudding

125 g (4 oz)
 self-raising flour
50 g (2 oz) fresh
 white breadcrumbs
pinch of salt
75 g (3 oz) shredded
 suet
25 g (1 oz) caster
 sugar
125 g (4 oz) apple,
 peeled and finely
 chopped
125 g (4 oz) dates,
 chopped
grated rind of 1
 lemon
150 ml (¼ pint)
 milk
 (approximately)

Mix together the flour, breadcrumbs, salt, suet and sugar. Stir in the apple, dates and lemon rind. Make a well in the centre and add enough milk to give a soft dropping consistency. Transfer to a greased 900 ml (1½ pint) pudding basin, cover with greased foil, pleated down the centre, and tie up with string.

Place the basin in a steamer or large saucepan half-filled with boiling water. Cover and cook for 1½ to 2 hours, topping up the water as necessary.

Remove the foil and turn the pudding out onto a plate. Serve with custard.

**Serves 6**

# Apple Meringue

750 g (1½ lb)
   cooking apples,
   peeled, cored and
   sliced
50 g (2 oz)
   granulated sugar
   (approximately)
1 jam Swiss roll,
   sliced
grated rind and juice
   of 1 lemon
2 egg whites
125 g (4 oz) caster
   sugar

Put the apples in a saucepan with a
little water and granulated sugar to
taste. Bring to the boil and simmer
for about 15 minutes or until soft.
Work to a smooth purée in an
electric blender, or beat with a spoon
and then rub through a sieve.

Line the base of a 1.75 litre (3 pint)
soufflé dish with the Swiss roll.
Spoon over the lemon rind and juice.
Spread the apple purée over the top.

Whisk the egg whites until stiff.
Whisk in half the caster sugar, then
fold in the remainder.

Pile the meringue over the apple.
Bake in a preheated cool oven, 150°C
(300°F), Gas Mark 2, for 30 minutes
until the meringue is golden. Serve
hot.

**Serves 4 to 6**

# Plum Flan

PASTRY:
175 g (6 oz) plain
   flour
25 g (1 oz) caster
   sugar
40 g (1½ oz)
   margarine
40 g (1½ oz) lard
1-2 tablespoons water
FILLING:
1 tablespoon
   digestive biscuit
   crumbs
500 g (1 lb) dessert
   plums, halved and
   stoned
50 g (2 oz) soft
   brown sugar
½ teaspoon ground
   cinnamon
25 g (1 oz) flaked
   almonds (optional)

Prepare and bake the pastry case as
for Savoury Leek Flan (see page 60),
replacing the salt with the caster
sugar.

Sprinkle the biscuit crumbs in the
cooked pastry case and arrange the
plum halves on top, skin side
upwards, overlapping if necessary.

Mix together the sugar, cinnamon
and flaked almonds, if using, and
sprinkle over the plums.

Bake in a hot oven, 220°C (425°F),
Gas Mark 7, for 40 minutes. Serve
hot or cold, with cream.

**Makes one 20 cm (8 inch) flan**

# Chocolate and Pineapple Upside-Down Pudding

1 x 227 g (8 oz) can
   pineapple slices
2-3 tablespoons
   golden syrup
125 g (4 oz) butter
   or margarine
125 g (4 oz) caster
   sugar
2 eggs, beaten
125 g (4 oz)
   self-raising flour
25 g (1 oz) cocoa

Drain the pineapple slices, reserving the syrup. Pour the golden syrup into a greased 18 cm (7 inch) round cake tin and arrange the pineapple slices on top.

Cream together the fat and sugar until fluffy, then beat in the eggs a little at a time. Sift the flour and cocoa together, then fold into the mixture, adding about 1 tablespoon of the reserved pineapple syrup, to give a smooth dropping consistency.

Spread the mixture over the pineapple and bake in a preheated moderate oven, 180°C (350°F), Gas Mark 4, for about 45 minutes.

Invert onto a plate. Warm the reserved syrup and serve separately.

**Serves 4 to 6**

# BAKING

## Meringues

2 large egg whites
125 g (4 oz) caster
    sugar
170 ml (6 fl oz)
    double cream,
    whipped with
    1 tablespoon caster
    sugar

Put the egg whites in a large mixing bowl and whisk until stiff. Whisk in 2 tablespoons of the sugar. Fold in the remaining sugar with a metal spoon.

Put the mixture into a piping bag fitted with 1 cm (½ inch) plain nozzle and pipe 16 rounds on a baking sheet lined with oiled greaseproof paper or non-stick parchment.

Bake in a very cool oven, 120°C (225°F), Gas Mark ¼, for about 3 hours or until the meringues are firm to the touch. Leave on the baking sheet until completely cold.

Sandwich the meringues together in pairs with cream just before serving.
**Makes 8**

# Cocoa Biscuits

125 g (4 oz) butter
or margarine
50 g (2 oz) caster
sugar
150 g (5 oz) plain
flour
1 tablespoon cocoa

Cream together the fat and sugar, then sift and stir in the flour and cocoa. Roll the mixture into small balls and place well apart on greased baking sheets. Flatten the balls slightly.

Bake in a preheated moderate oven, 160°C (325°F), Gas Mark 3, for 30 minutes. Leave on the baking sheets for a few minutes, then transfer to a wire rack to cool.

**Makes about 20**

# Jam Faces

250 g (8 oz) butter
    or margarine
250 g (8 oz) caster
    sugar
2 eggs, beaten
few drops of vanilla
    essence
500 g (1 lb) plain
    flour, sifted
jam for spreading

Cream together the fat and sugar, then gradually beat in the eggs and vanilla essence. Stir in the flour and mix to a fairly soft dough.

Turn onto a lightly floured board and knead gently. Roll out to about 3 mm (⅛ inch) thickness and cut into rounds with a 6 cm (2½ inch) pastry cutter. From half of these, remove two rounds to represent eyes, using a 1 cm (½ inch) cutter, then make a slit for the mouth.

Place all the biscuits on greased baking sheets and bake in a preheated moderately hot oven, 190°C (375°F), Gas Mark 5, for about 15 minutes or until golden brown. Leave on the baking sheets for a few minutes, then transfer to a wire rack to cool.

When cold, spread the plain biscuits with jam and put the faces on top.
**Makes about 20**

# Shortbread

150 g (5 oz) plain
  flour
pinch of salt
1 teaspoon ground
  cinnamon
25 g (1 oz) ground
  rice
50 g (2 oz) caster
  sugar
125 g (4 oz) butter,
  chilled
caster sugar for
  dredging

Sift the flour, salt, cinnamon and rice into a mixing bowl. Stir in the sugar. Rub in the butter until the mixture resembles breadcrumbs. Knead until smooth but not sticky. Wrap in foil and chill in the refrigerator for 30 minutes.

Press the dough out to an 18 cm (7 inch) round and place on a greased baking sheet. Flute the edge and prick all over with a fork. Mark into 8 portions and chill for 30 minutes.

Bake in a preheated moderate oven, 160°C (325°F), Gas Mark 3, for about 40 minutes or until pale golden. Leave on the baking sheet for 10 minutes, then transfer to a wire rack to cool completely. Sprinkle with sugar and break into portions to serve.

**Makes 8**

# Moist Fruit Cake

175 g (6 oz) raisins
175 g (6 oz)
  sultanas
175 g (6 oz) currants
250 g (8 oz) soft
  brown sugar
1/2 teaspoon ground
  cinnamon
1/2 teaspoon ground
  ginger
175 g (6 oz) butter
  or margarine
250 ml (8 fl oz)
  water
3 eggs, beaten
150 g (5 oz) plain
  flour
150 g (5 oz)
  self-raising flour
1/2 teaspoon
  bicarbonate of soda
50 g (2 oz) glacé
  cherries, chopped
50 g (2 oz) mixed
  peel
50 g (2 oz) walnuts,
  chopped

Put the raisins, sultanas, currants, sugar, spices and butter or margarine into a saucepan with the water. Bring to the boil, stirring. Simmer for 3 minutes then leave to cool. When cold, stir in the eggs.

Sift the flours and bicarbonate of soda into a mixing bowl and stir in the cherries, peel and nuts. Stir in the fruit and egg mixture until thoroughly mixed, then turn into a lined and greased 23 cm (9 inch) round cake tin.

Bake in a preheated moderate oven, 160°C (325°F), Gas Mark 3, for 1 1/2 to 1 3/4 hours. Turn out and cool on a wire rack.
**Makes one 23 cm (9 inch) cake**

# No-Bake Chocolate Cake

50 g (2 oz) butter
125 g (4 oz) plain
  chocolate, chopped
2 tablespoons golden
  syrup
125 g (4 oz) petit
  beurre type
  biscuits, crumbled
25 g (1 oz) glacé
  cherries, chopped
25 g (1 oz) dates,
  chopped
25 g (1 oz)
  desiccated coconut
1/2 orange

Melt the butter and chocolate in a saucepan with the syrup. Stir in the biscuits, cherries, dates and coconut. Spoon into a greased shallow 15 cm (6 inch) square cake tin and press down firmly, using the cut side of the orange. Leave to set, then cut into squares.
**Makes 16 squares**

# One-Stage Victoria Sandwich

CAKE MIXTURE:
*125 g (4 oz) soft
   margarine*
*125 g (4 oz) caster
   sugar*
*2 eggs*
*125 g (4 oz)
   self-raising flour*
*1 teaspoon baking
   powder*
FILLING AND
   TOPPING:
*jam or buttercream
   icing (see Butterfly
   Cakes)*
*crystallized orange
   or lemon slices to
   decorate (optional)*

Place all the cake ingredients in a bowl and beat thoroughly for 2 minutes until smooth, using an electric beater if possible.

Divide the mixture between two lined and greased 18 cm (7 inch) sandwich tins and bake in a preheated moderate oven, 160°C (325°F), Gas Mark 3, for 30 to 35 minutes until the cakes are golden and springy to the touch. Turn out and cool on a wire rack.

Sandwich together with jam or buttercream icing. Spread more icing over the top and decorate with orange slices if liked.
**Makes one 18 cm (7 inch) cake**
VARIATIONS: Any of the following can be added to the basic ingredients: few drops vanilla or almond essence;
1 tablespoon cocoa dissolved in 2
   tablespoons hot water;
2 teaspoons instant coffee dissolved
   in 1 tablespoon hot water.

# Butterfly Cakes

One-stage Victoria
    Sandwich
    mixture, plain,
    chocolate or
    coffee-flavoured
    (see opposite)
BUTTERCREAM
    ICING:
75 g (3 oz) butter,
    softened
175 g (6 oz) icing
    sugar, sifted
1-2 tablespoons
    warm water
flavouring (see note)
TO DECORATE:
icing sugar, sifted

Divide the mixture between about 20
greased bun tins.

Bake in a preheated moderately
hot oven, 190°C (375°F), Gas Mark
5, for about 15 minutes until golden
brown and firm. Transfer to a wire
rack to cool.

To make the icing, beat together
the butter, icing sugar and warm
water until well mixed. Stir in the
flavouring.

Cut a slice off the top of each cake
and pipe or spoon in a little icing.
Cut the slices in half and replace on
the cakes to resemble butterfly
wings. Sprinkle with icing sugar.

**Makes about 20**

NOTE: Flavour the icing with any of
the following:

few drops vanilla or almond essence;
1 tablespoon cocoa dissolved in a
    little hot water;
2 teaspoons instant coffee dissolved
    in a little hot water.

# Honey Gingerbread

250 g (8 oz) plain
  flour
½ teaspoon
  bicarbonate of soda
125 g (4 oz) clear
  honey
125 g (4 oz) black
  treacle
50 g (2 oz) golden
  syrup
50 g (2 oz) soft
  brown sugar
125 g (4 oz) butter
  or margarine
3 teaspoons ground
  ginger
½ teaspoon ground
  cinnamon
120 ml (4 fl oz)
  milk
2 eggs, beaten
chopped nuts to
  decorate (optional)

Sift the flour and bicarbonate of soda into a bowl; make a well in the centre. Place the honey, treacle, syrup, sugar, butter or margarine, spices and milk in a saucepan and heat gently, stirring. Cool slightly, then beat in the eggs. Pour into the flour and beat well.

Turn into a lined and greased 20 cm (8 inch) square cake tin. Sprinkle a few chopped nuts over the top, if liked. Bake in a preheated moderate oven, 160°C (325°F), Gas Mark 3, for 1½ hours. Turn out onto a wire rack to cool

**Makes one 20 cm (8 inch) cake**

# Banana Teabread

125 g (4 oz) butter
  or margarine
125 g (4 oz) caster
  sugar
2 eggs
500 g (1 lb)
  bananas, mashed
250 g (8 oz)
  self-raising flour
½ teaspoon
  bicarbonate of soda

Cream together the butter or margarine and the sugar. Beat in the eggs, one at a time, then the bananas. Sift the flour and bicarbonate of soda together and fold into the mixture.

Turn into a greased 1 kg (2 lb) loaf tin and bake in a preheated moderate oven, 180°C (350°F), Gas Mark 4, for 1¼ hours. Turn out and cool on a wire rack.

Store overnight in an airtight tin, then serve sliced and buttered.

**Makes one 1 kg (2 lb) loaf**

# Date and Walnut Teabread

250 g (8 oz)
  self-raising flour
½ teaspoon ground
  mixed spice
50 g (2 oz) walnuts,
  chopped
125 g (4 oz) dates,
  chopped
5 tablespoons milk
25 g (1 oz) soft
  brown sugar
2 tablespoons malt
  extract
2 tablespoons golden
  syrup

Sift together the flour and spice, then stir in the walnuts and dates. Place the milk, sugar, malt and syrup in a saucepan and warm gently, then beat into the dry ingredients.

Turn into a greased 500 g (1 lb) loaf tin and bake in a preheated moderate oven, 160°C (325°F), Gas Mark 3, for 50 minutes to 1 hour. Turn onto a wire rack to cool.

**Makes one 500 g (1 lb) loaf**

# Farmhouse Bread

25 g (1 oz) fresh
  yeast
900 ml (1½ pints)
  warm water
1.5 kg (3 lb) strong
  plain white flour
1 tablespoon salt
25 g (1 oz) lard

Blend the yeast with one third of the water.

Sift the flour and salt into a large bowl and rub in the lard. Make a well in the centre and pour in the yeast liquid plus the remaining water. Mix to a smooth dough, then work with one hand until the dough leaves the sides of the bowl clean.

Turn onto a lighly floured surface and knead for 10 minutes until smooth and elastic. Place in a clean bowl, cover with a piece of oiled plastic wrap and leave to rise in a warm place for about 1 hour until doubled in size.

Turn onto a floured surface and knead for 2 to 3 minutes. Divide the dough into 4 and place in 4 greased and floured 500 g (1 lb) loaf tins. Make a deep cut along each loaf. Cover and leave to rise until the dough reaches the top of the tins.

Bake in a preheated hot oven, 230°C (450°F), Gas Mark 8, for 30 to 40 minutes or until the bread has shrunk from the sides of the tins and sounds hollow when tapped. Turn onto a wire rack to cool.
**Makes four 500 g (1 lb) loaves**

# Crusty Rolls

15 g (½ oz) fresh
  yeast
450 ml (¾ pint)
  warm water
750 g (1½ lb) strong
  plain white flour
1½ teaspoons salt
15 g (½ oz) lard
milk to glaze

Make the dough and leave to rise once (as above). Turn out and knead for 2 to 3 minutes, then divide into 18 pieces. Shape into rounds and place 2.5 cm (1 inch) apart on floured baking sheets. Cover with a piece of oiled plastic wrap and leave to rise until the rounds have doubled in size.

Brush with a little milk and bake in a preheated hot oven, 230°C (450°F), Gas Mark 8, for 20 minutes. Transfer to a wire rack to cool.
**Makes 18**

# One–Rise Brown Bread

50 g (2 oz) fresh
  yeast
900 ml (1½ pints)
  water
750 g (1½ lb)
  wholewheat flour
750 g (1½ lb) strong
  plain white flour
1 tablespoon salt
15 g (½ oz) lard
2 tablespoons sugar
TOPPING:
lightly salted water
crushed cornflakes

Make the dough as for Farmhouse
bread (see opposite), stirring the
sugar into the flour mixture before
adding the yeast.

Knead for 10 minutes then divide
in half and place in 2 greased and
floured 1 kg (2 lb) loaf tins. Cover
with a piece of oiled plastic wrap and
leave to rise in a warm place for
about 30 minutes until doubled in
size. Brush with salted water and
sprinkle with cornflakes.

Bake in a preheated hot oven,
230°C (450°F), Gas Mark 8, for 15
minutes, then lower the heat to
200°C (400°F), Gas Mark 6, and bake
for a further 45 minutes or until the
loaves sound hollow when tapped.
Turn onto a wire rack to cool.
**Makes two 1 kg (2 lb) loaves**

# Teatime Scones

250 g (8 oz)
  self-raising flour
½ teaspoon baking
  powder
50 g (2 oz) butter or
  margarine
2 tablespoons caster
  sugar
75 g (3 oz) mixed
  dried fruit
150 ml (¼ pint)
  milk
  (approximately)

Sift the flour and baking powder into a bowl. Rub in the fat until the mixture resembles breadcrumbs, then stir in the sugar and fruit. Add enough milk to give a fairly soft dough.

Turn onto a lightly floured surface, knead very gently then roll out to a 2 cm (¾ inch) thickness. Cut into 5 cm (2 inch) rounds and place on a lightly floured baking sheet. Brush with milk and bake in a preheated hot oven, 220°C (425°F), Gas Mark 7, for 10 minutes. Cool on a wire rack.

Cut in half and spread with butter and jam to serve.
**Makes 10 to 12**

# Savoury Scones

250 g (8 oz)
  self-raising flour
½ teaspoon baking
  powder
pinch of salt
1 teaspoon mustard
  powder
50 g (2 oz) butter or
  margarine
75 g (3 oz) Cheddar
  cheese, finely
  grated
50 g (2 oz) sliced
  ham, diced
150 ml (¼ pint)
  milk
  (approximately)

Sift the flour, baking powder, salt and mustard powder into a bowl. Rub in the fat until the mixture resembles breadcrumbs, then stir in the cheese and ham. Add enough milk to give a fairly soft dough.

Turn onto a lightly floured surface, knead very gently then roll out to a 2 cm (¾ inch) thickness. Cut into 5 cm (2 inch) rounds and place on a lightly floured baking sheet. Brush with milk and bake in a preheated hot oven, 220°C (425°F), Gas Mark 7, for 10 minutes. Cool on a wire rack.

Cut in half and spread with butter to serve.
**Makes 10 to 12**

# INDEX